# FRIDGE CAKES

*over 30 no-bake desserts*

**JEAN-LUC SADY**

PHOTOGRAPHY BY ISABELLE KANAKO

**hardie grant** books

# CONTENTS

# THE BASICS

### THE RECIPE

Fridge cakes are cakes made of biscuits and whipped cream built up in layers in a mould, simply chilled then turned out. Few ingredients are required (biscuits, whipping cream, mascarpone, and some extra toppings), they take less than 30 minutes to make and you won't need to turn the oven on!

### THE ESSENTIAL INGREDIENT: WHIPPED CREAM

To make the perfect whipped cream for these cakes, mix whipping cream with either mascarpone or cream cheese. This will give you a thick whipped cream, which will prevent the cake from collapsing when you assemble or unmould it. After 4 hours in the fridge, the cake will be firm and easy to slice, without the need for gelatine.

All the ingredients need to be very cold. Chill mascarpone, cream cheese and fromage frais in the fridge before use. Put cream in the freezer for 25–30 minutes: when it begins to crystallise slightly around the edges, you can be sure that your whipped cream will be a success.

### THE STRUCTURE: THE BISCUITS

Use thin biscuits: shortbread, coconut, chocolate, digestives, speculaas (spiced biscuits). They need to absorb the moistness of the cream without softening completely or losing their texture.

### ASSEMBLING THE CAKE

Line the mould with cling film (plastic wrap) and assemble the cake upside down: a layer of cream at the base topped with a layer of biscuits. The finished cake will sit on a biscuit base. To turn out, place a plate on top of the mould and turn the whole lot upside down. The cling film will peel away without sticking to the cream.

To ensure you finish with a cake that is completely covered in cream, when you are assembling the layers, make sure that the biscuits don't touch the edges of the mould.

### THE MOULD

You can use all sorts of moulds: a loaf tin, springform cake tin, charlotte mould, gratin dish or freezer-proof plastic container. You can also choose not to turn out the cake but to serve it in its dish; for this, you'll need to reverse the order of assembly, starting with the biscuit and finishing with the cream.

# STRABERRY

## & SUGARED ALMONDS

20 MIN     20 CM (8 IN) ROUND CAKE TIN     4 H

### CAKE

400 ml (14 fl oz) whipping cream

300 g (10½ oz) strawberries

300 g (10½ oz) mascarpone

70 g (2½ oz) caster (superfine) sugar

300 g (10½ oz) cereal biscuits

### TOPPING

120 g (4 oz) strawberry jam

60 g (2 oz) sugared almonds, crushed

Pour the cream into a large bowl and place in the freezer for 30 minutes.

Hull the strawberries and chop them into small pieces.

Using an electric whisk or a food processor, whip the mascarpone and chilled cream together until thick. Gradually whisk in the sugar.

Line the tin with cling film (plastic wrap). Spread a third of the cream in the bottom. Sprinkle with a third of the chopped strawberries. Cover with a third of the biscuits, ensuring that they don't touch the sides. Repeat these layers twice more. Refrigerate for at least 4 hours.

Turn the cake out onto a plate. Cover with strawberry jam and decorate with pieces of sugared almonds.

fruit

# RASPBERRY
## & SPICED BISCUIT

25 MIN    CHARLOTTE MOULD    4 H

### CAKE
400 ml (14 fl oz) whipping cream

400 g (14 oz) mascarpone

80 g (2 ¾ oz) caster (superfine) sugar

200 g (7 oz) raspberries

500 g (1 lb 2 oz) speculaas (spiced biscuits)

### TOPPING
a few fresh raspberries

2 speculaas, crushed

Pour the cream into a large bowl and place in the freezer for 30 minutes.

Using an electric whisk or a food processor, whip the mascarpone and chilled cream together until thick. Gradually whisk in the sugar. Once the cream is firm, gently stir in the raspberries.

Line the mould with cling film (plastic wrap). Spread half the cream in the bottom. Cover with half the biscuits, ensuring that they don't touch the sides. Repeat these layers. Refrigerate for at least 4 hours.

Turn the cake out onto a plate. Decorate the top with raspberries and crushed biscuits.

# APRICOT
## & HONEY

30 MIN    CHARLOTTE MOULD    4 H

### CAKE

250 ml (9 fl oz) whipping cream

3 gelatine leaves

75 g (2 ½ oz) honey

250 g (9 oz) fromage frais

300 g (10 ½ oz) apricot purée (frozen)

250 g (9 oz) speculaas (spiced biscuits)

### TOPPING

3 tinned apricot halves, cut into slices

1 speculaas, crushed

Pour the cream into a large bowl and place in the freezer for 30 minutes.

Soak the gelatine in a little cold water and mix the honey into the fromage frais.

Put the apricot purée into a pan and bring to the boil. Turn off the heat. Squeeze any excess water from the soaked gelatine leaves and stir into the apricot purée and then mix into the fromage frais.

Line the mould with cling film (plastic wrap). Line the edges of the mould with biscuits. Spread a third of the apricot cream in the bottom of the mould. Cover with a third of the biscuits. Repeat these layers twice more. Refrigerate for at least 4 hours.

Whip the cold whipping cream using an electric whisk or a food processor until thick. Turn the cake out onto a plate. Using a spatula, cover the top and sides of the cake with the whipped cream. Chill.

Decorate with apricot slices and crushed biscuits.

### CHEF'S TIP

For this recipe, you have to cover the cake with cream once it has been removed from the mould because you can't pour the hot apricot cream over the whipped cream in the mould.

fruit

# PINEAPPLE

## & WHITE CHOCOLATE

25 MN     20 CM (8 IN)     4 H
ROUND CAKE TIN

### CAKE

300 ml (10 fl oz) whipping cream

400 g (14 oz) mascarpone

70 g (2½ oz) caster (superfine) sugar

6 tinned pineapple slices

300 g (10½ oz) cereal biscuits

### TOPPING

150 g (5 oz) white chocolate

desiccated coconut

Pour the cream into a large bowl and place in the freezer for 30 minutes.

Using an electric whisk or a food processor, whip the mascarpone and chilled cream together until thick. Gradually whisk in the sugar.

Line the tin with cling film (plastic wrap). Drain the pineapple slices between two sheets of kitchen paper. Lay the slices in the bottom of the tin and cover with one third of the cream. Add a third of the biscuits, ensuring that they don't touch the side of the tin, then cover with more cream. Repeat twice more, finishing with a layer of biscuits. Refrigerate for at least 4 hours.

Prepare the topping by melting the white chocolate in a bain-marie.

Turn the cake out onto a plate. Sprinkle with some desiccated coconut, then drizzle lines of the melted white chocolate over the top.

fruit

# BANANA

## CITRUS & COCONUT

35 MIN     GRATIN DISH     4 H

### CAKE

300 ml (10 fl oz) whipping cream

400 g (14 oz) mascarpone

70 g (2 ½ oz) caster (superfine) sugar

zest of 1 orange

zest of 1 lemon

500 g (1 lb 2 oz) coconut cookies

### BANANA AND ORANGE CREAM

100 g (3 ½ oz) bananas

40 g (1 ½ oz) caster (superfine) sugar

15 g (½ oz) plain (all-purpose) flour

3 eggs, beaten

200 ml (7 fl oz) orange juice

1 tablespoon lemon juice

### TOPPING

1 banana

50 g (2 oz) coconut cookies

Pour the cream into a large bowl and place in the freezer for 30 minutes.

Prepare the banana and orange cream by mixing all the ingredients together. Pour into a saucepan and heat over a low heat, stirring constantly, until thickened. Leave to cool and set aside.

Using an electric whisk or a food processor, whip the mascarpone and chilled cream together until thick. Gradually whisk in the sugar then stir in the orange and lemon zest.

Layer half of the cookies in the bottom of the mould. Top with half of the banana and orange cream, followed by half of the whipped cream. Repeat these layers. Refrigerate for at least 4 hours.

Just before serving, slice the banana and crush the coconut cookies. Arrange the banana slices over the top and sprinkle with cookie crumbs.

### CHEF'S TIP

If you want to turn the cake out, line the dish with cling film (plastic wrap) and layer the ingredients in the reverse order, starting with a layer of cream and finishing with cookies.

fruit

# PEACH
## LEMON & PINE NUT

20 MIN        20 CM (8 IN)        4 H
              ROUND CAKE TIN

### CAKE

350 ml (12 fl oz) whipping cream

350 g (12 oz) mascarpone

zest of 1 lemon

70 g (2 ½ oz) caster (superfine) sugar

300 g (10 ½ oz) tinned peaches in syrup, drained and diced

500 g (1 lb 2 oz) cereal biscuits

### TOPPING

100 g (3 ½ oz) pine nuts, toasted

Pour the cream into a large bowl and place in the freezer for 30 minutes.

Mix the mascarpone with the chilled cream and most of the lemon zest (reserve a little for the topping). Using an electric whisk or a food processor, whip until thick. Gradually whisk in the sugar. Carefully stir in the diced peaches.

Line the tin with cling film (plastic wrap). Pour a third of the peach cream into the bottom of the mould. Cover with a third of the biscuits, ensuring that they don't touch the sides. Repeat these layers twice. Refrigerate for at least 4 hours.

Turn the cake out onto a plate. Scatter over the toasted pine nuts and reserved lemon zest.

# MANGO
## & PASSION FRUIT

20 MIN    SQUARE OR RECTANGULAR    4 H
PLASTIC CONTAINER

### CAKE

300 ml (10 fl oz) whipping cream

400 g (14 oz) mascarpone

70 g (2 1/2 oz) caster (superfine) sugar

500 g (1 lb 2 oz) digestive or cereal biscuits

### TOPPING

2 mangoes

3 passion fruits

Pour the cream into a large bowl and place in the freezer for 30 minutes.

Using an electric whisk or a food processor, whip the mascarpone and chilled cream together until thick. Gradually whisk in the sugar.

Line the mould with cling film (plastic wrap). Spread a third of the cream in the bottom. Cover with a third of the biscuits, ensuring that they don't touch the sides. Repeat these layers twice. Refrigerate for at least 4 hours.

Turn the cake out onto a plate. Peel the mango and remove the stone. Cut or peel the flesh into thin slices and arrange on top of the cake. Scoop out the flesh and seeds of the passion fruits and sprinkle over the top of the mango.

fruit

# PEAR
## & ORANGE

25 MIN

CHARLOTTE MOULD

4 H

### CAKE

200 ml (7 fl oz) whipping cream

200 g (7 oz) cream cheese

zest of 1 orange

50 g (2 oz) caster (superfine) sugar

130 g (4 ½ oz) tinned pears in syrup, drained and diced

170 g (6 oz) digestive biscuits or graham crackers

### TOPPING

200 g (7 oz) dark chocolate, broken into pieces

50 g (2 oz) whole almonds, roughly chopped

½ tinned pear in syrup, drained and diced

Pour the cream into a large bowl and place in the freezer for 30 minutes.

Using an electric whisk or a food processor, whip together the cream cheese, cream and orange zest until thick. Gradually whisk in the sugar. Transfer a third of this cream mixture to another bowl and stir in the diced pears. Set aside.

Line the mould with cling film (plastic wrap). Spread a layer of cream in the bottom, then cover with a quarter of the biscuits, ensuring that they don't touch the sides. Repeat these two layers, then pour over the cream and pear mixture. Finish with a biscuit layer. Refrigerate for at least 4 hours.

Melt the chocolate in a bain-marie. Turn the cake out onto a plate. Pour the melted chocolate over the top of the cake, then scatter with almonds and diced pear.

# APPLE
## & MAPLE SYRUP

30 MIN    CHARLOTTE MOULD    4 H

### CAKE

450 ml (15 fl oz) whipping cream

350 g (12 oz) cream cheese

80 g (2 ¾ oz) caster (superfine) sugar

500 g (1 lb 2 oz) speculaas (spiced biscuits)

### TOPPING

4 tablespoons maple syrup

1 large eating apple

Pour the cream into a large bowl and place in the freezer for 30 minutes.

Using an electric whisk or a food processor, whip the cream cheese and chilled cream together until thick. Gradually whisk in the sugar.

Line the mould with cling film (plastic wrap). Spread a third of the cream in the bottom. Cover with a third of the biscuits, ensuring that they don't touch the sides. Repeat twice more. Refrigerate for at least 4 hours.

Prepare the topping by pouring the maple syrup into a pan. Peel, core and dice the apple. Add it to the pan and cook over a low heat for about 10 minutes. The apple should be cooked but still firm. Leave the topping to cool.

Turn the cake out onto a plate and cover with the diced apple in maple syrup.

# BLUEBERRY

## & CEREAL BISCUIT

20 MIN   20 CM (8 IN) ROUND CAKE TIN   4 H

### CAKE

400 ml (14 fl oz) whipping cream

300 g (10 ½ oz) mascarpone

70 g (2 ½ oz) caster (superfine) sugar

300 g (10 ½ oz) cereal biscuits

### TOPPING

150 g (5 oz) blueberry jam

a few blueberries

3 cereal biscuits, crumbled, or 3 slices of gingerbread, diced

Pour the cream into a large bowl and place in the freezer for 30 minutes.

Using an electric whisk or a food processor, whip the mascarpone and chilled cream together until thick. Gradually whisk in the sugar.

Line the mould with cling film (plastic wrap). Spread a third of the cream in the bottom. Add a third of the biscuits, ensuring that they don't touch the side of the tin. Repeat these layers twice. Refrigerate for at least 4 hours.

Blend the jam to a purée. Turn the cake out onto a plate, cover the top with the jam and scatter over the blueberries and crumbled biscuits or diced gingerbread.

*fruit*

# BLACKCURRANT
## & GINGERBREAD

30 MIN    GRATIN DISH OR SQUARE CAKE TIN    4 H

### CAKE

300 ml (10 fl oz) whipping cream

500 g (1 lb 2 oz) cream cheese

80 g (2 3/4 oz) caster (superfine) sugar

30 g (1 oz) gingerbread, broken into pieces

300 g (10 1/2 oz) blackcurrant jam

200 g (7 oz) shortbread or digestive biscuits

### TOPPING

200 ml (7 fl oz) light pouring custard

1 slice of gingerbread

1 tablespoon blackcurrant jam

Pour the cream into a large bowl and place in the freezer for 30 minutes.

Using an electric whisk or a food processor, whip the cream cheese and chilled cream together until thick. Gradually whisk in the sugar.

Mix the gingerbread into the jam by crushing it with a fork. Spread the shortbread or digestive biscuits with this mixture and sandwich them together in three equal-sized columns.

Line the dish or tin with cling film (plastic wrap). Spread a layer of the cream in the bottom. Lay the three columns of biscuits horizontally on the cream layer, making sure they don't touch the edges of the dish. Cover with the remainder of the cream. Refrigerate for at least 4 hours.

Turn the cake out onto a plate and pour over the custard. Spread the gingerbread with the blackcurrant jam and cut into small squares. Scatter over the top of the cake.

*fruit*

# CHERRY

## & AMARETTO

25 MIN

PLASTIC BOWL

4 H

### CAKE

300 ml (10 fl oz) whipping cream

250 g (9 oz) mascarpone

180 g (6 oz) cream cheese

90 g (3 oz) caster (superfine) sugar

3 tablespoons amaretto

150 g (5 oz) pitted cherries (fresh or in syrup)

150 g (5 oz) shortbread or digestive biscuits

### TOPPING

1 packet of chocolate crêpe dentelle biscuits (or other luxury chocolate wafers)

Pour the cream into a large bowl and place in the freezer for 30 minutes.

Using an electric whisk or a food processor, whip the mascarpone, cream cheese and chilled cream together until thick. Gradually whisk in the sugar, then stir in the amaretto.

Line the mould with cling film (plastic wrap). Coat the inside of the bowl completely with the cream mixture. Lay some biscuits in the base and cover with cream. Top with half the cherries. Repeat these layers. Cover with more cream and finish with a layer of biscuits. Refrigerate for at least 4 hours.

Turn the cake out onto a plate. Gently crumble the wafers and scatter them over the top.

fruit

# APPLE CIDER
## & CARAMEL

1 H    GRATIN DISH    2 H

### CAKE

300 ml (10 fl oz) whipping cream

3 apples

20 g ($^3/_4$ oz) salted butter, cut into small pieces

4 teaspoons vanilla extract

100 ml (3 $^1/_2$ fl oz) sweet cider

300 g (10 $^1/_2$ oz) cream cheese

60 g (2 oz) caster (superfine) sugar

300 g (10 $^1/_2$ oz) Viennese whirls

### TOPPING

100 g (3 $^1/_2$ oz) salted caramel sauce
1 shortbread biscuit, crumbled

Pour the cream into a large bowl and place in the freezer for 30 minutes.

Preheat the oven to 180°C (350°F/Gas 4).

Core and peel the apples and lay them in an ovenproof dish. Scatter over the butter and sprinkle over the vanilla extract. Pour over the cider and bake in the oven for 30–40 minutes, until the apples are tender. Crush with a fork and leave to cool.

Using an electric whisk or a food processor, whip the cream cheese and chilled cream together until thick. Gradually whisk in the sugar.

Lay half the Viennese whirls out in the bottom of the mould, followed by half the apple, then half the cream. Repeat these layers. Refrigerate for at least 4 hours.

Warm the caramel sauce and drizzle it over the top of the cake. Scatter with the biscuit crumbs.

### CHEF'S TIP

If you want to turn the cake out, line the dish with cling film (plastic wrap) and layer the ingredients in the reverse order, starting with a layer of the cream and finishing with the biscuits.

fruit

# APRICOT

## & BROWNIE

30 MIN

GRATIN DISH

4 H

### CAKE

300 ml (10 fl oz) whipping cream

400 g (14 oz) cream cheese

70 g (2½ oz) caster (superfine) sugar

2 tablespoons orange blossom water

200 g (7 oz) tinned apricot halves in syrup, drained and diced

150 g (5 oz) brownie, diced

150 g (5 oz) chocolate cookies

### TOPPING

150 g (5 oz) dark chocolate

2 apricot halves, diced

Pour the cream into a large bowl and place in the freezer for 30 minutes.

Using an electric whisk or a food processor, whip the cream cheese and chilled cream together until thick. Gradually whisk in the sugar. Stir in the orange blossom water.

Divide the mixture into two equal portions. Stir the diced apricots into one portion and the diced brownie into the other.

Line the dish with cling film (plastic wrap). Spread the brownie cream in the bottom. Cover with half the chocolate cookies, ensuring that they don't touch the sides. Spread the apricot cream over the top and finish with a layer of cookies. Refrigerate for at least 4 hours.

Turn the cake out onto a plate. Shave the chocolate using a vegetable peeler and scatter over the top along with the diced apricot.

# CHOCO FUDGE
## & OREO®

25 MN     20 CM (8 IN)     4 H
ROUND CAKE TIN

### CAKE

200 ml (7 fl oz) whipping cream

300 g (10 1/2 oz) cream cheese

50 g (2 oz) caster (superfine) sugar

210 g (7 1/2 oz) Oreo® biscuits

### TOPPING

60 ml (2 fl oz) whipping cream

20 g (3/4 oz) butter

30 g (1 oz) honey

70 g (2 1/2 oz) dark chocolate, broken into pieces

Pour the cream into a large bowl and place in the freezer for 25 minutes.

Using an electric whisk or a food processor, whip the cream cheese and chilled cream together until thick. Gradually whisk in the sugar.

Line the tin with cling film (plastic wrap). Spread a third of the cream in the bottom of the mould, then add a third of the Oreo® biscuits, making sure they don't touch the edges. Repeat these layers twice. Refrigerate for at least 4 hours.

Prepare the topping. Put the cream, butter and honey in a pan and bring to the boil. Remove the pan from the heat, add the chocolate and stir until smooth. Leave to cool slightly.

Turn the cake out onto a plate and pour over the chocolate sauce.

chocolate

# CHOCOLATE CHIP
## & SPICED BISCUIT

25 MIN          GRATIN DISH          4 H

### CAKE

300 ml (10 fl oz) whipping cream

500 g (1 lb 2 oz) mascarpone

80 g (2 ¾ oz) caster (superfine) sugar

100 g (3 ½ oz) chocolate chips

500 g (1 lb 2 oz) speculaas (spiced biscuits)

### TOPPING

1 tablespoon chocolate chips

Pour the cream into a large bowl and place in the freezer for 30 minutes.

Using an electric whisk or a food processor, whip the mascarpone and chilled cream together until thick. Gradually whisk in the sugar, then gently stir in the chocolate chips.

Line the dish with cling film (plastic wrap). Spread a third of the cream in the bottom. Cover with a third of the biscuits, ensuring that they don't touch the sides. Repeat these layers twice. Refrigerate for at least 4 hours.

Turn the cake out onto a plate. Sprinkle the chocolate chips on top.

# WHITE CHOCOLATE
## & LIME

30 MIN     RECTANGULAR PLASTIC     4 H
CONTAINER

### CAKE

300 ml (10 fl oz) whipping cream

zest of 2 limes

300 g (10 ½ oz) white chocolate, broken into pieces

200 g (7 oz) digestive or cereal biscuits

### TOPPING

50 g (2 oz) coconut flakes

zest of 1 lime

Put the cream and lime zest in a pan and bring to the boil. Remove from the heat and stir in the white chocolate until you have a creamy ganache. Leave to cool completely and then refrigerate for at least 2 hours.

Using an electric whisk or in a food processor, whisk the chilled white chocolate and lime ganache until thick.

Line the mould with cling film (plastic wrap). Spread a third of the ganache in a layer covering the bottom. Cover with a third of the biscuits, ensuring that they don't touch the sides. Repeat these layers twice. Refrigerate for at least 4 hours.

Turn the cake out onto a plate and sprinkle the coconut flakes and lime zest on top.

chocolate

# CHOCOLATE
## ORANGE

25 MIN

LOAF TIN

4 H

### CAKE

550 ml (1 pint) whipping cream

350 g (12 oz) dark chocolate, broken into pieces

200 g (7 oz) cream cheese

40 g (1½ oz) caster (superfine) sugar

zest of 1 orange

350 g (12 oz) rich tea biscuits

### TOPPING

100 g (3½ oz) grated chocolate or chocolate vermicelli

Pour 200 ml (7 fl oz) of the cream into a large bowl and place in the freezer for 25 minutes.

Pour the rest of the cream into a saucepan and bring to the boil. Remove from the heat and stir in the chocolate until you have a creamy ganache. Set aside.

Using an electric whisk or a food processor, whip the cream cheese and chilled cream together until thick. Gradually whisk in the sugar and orange zest.

Line the tin with cling film (plastic wrap). Cover the base and sides with the cream. Add a layer of biscuits, ensuring that they don't touch the sides of the tin. Cover with ganache. Repeat, finishing with a layer of biscuits. Refrigerate for at least 4 hours.

Turn the cake out onto a plate and sprinkle the grated chocolate or chocolate vermicelli over the top.

# CHOCOLATE
## & MELBA RASPBERRIES

25 MIN      GRATIN DISH      4 H

### CAKE
350 ml (12 fl oz) whipping cream

2 vanilla pods, broken in half

350 g (12 oz) cream cheese

80 g (2 ³/₄ oz) caster (superfine) sugar

500 g (1 lb 2 oz) chocolate cookies

### MELBA RASPBERRIES
100 g (3 ¹/₂ oz) redcurrants

40 g (1 ¹/₂ oz) caster (superfine) sugar

200 g (7 oz) raspberries

Put the cream and vanilla pods in a saucepan and bring to the boil. Turn off the heat and leave the cream to cool completely. Pour into a large bowl and place in the freezer for 30 minutes.

Remove the vanilla pods from the chilled cream. Using an electric whisk or a food processor, whip the cream and cream cheese together until thick. Gradually whisk in the sugar.

Line the dish with cling film (plastic wrap). Cover the base with a quarter of the cream mixture. Add a quarter of the cookies in a layer on top, ensuring that they don't touch the side of the tin. Repeat these layers three times. Refrigerate for at least 4 hours.

To make the melba raspberries, first place the redcurrants and the sugar into a saucepan with 2 tablespoons of water, bring to the boil and boil for 2 minutes. Blend to a purée, then strain through a fine sieve. Leave to cool, then stir in the raspberries.

Turn the cake out onto a plate and cover with the melba raspberries.

# PEANUT BUTTER
## & DARK CHOCOLATE

30 MIN

LOAF TIN

4 H

### CAKE

400 ml (14 fl oz) whipping cream

200 g (7 oz) dark chocolate, broken into pieces

2 tablespoons peanut butter

200 g (7 oz) cream cheese

350 g (12 oz) digestive or cereal biscuits

### TOPPING

5 Oreo® biscuits, crumbled

Pour 200 ml (7 fl oz) of the cream into a large bowl and place in the freezer for 30 minutes.

Pour the rest of the cream into a saucepan and bring to the boil. Remove from the heat and stir in the chocolate until you have a creamy ganache. Stir in the peanut butter, then set aside.

Mix the cream cheese with the chilled cream. Whip, using an electric whisk or a food processor, until thick.

Line the tin with cling film (plastic wrap). Cover the base and sides with the cream. Add a layer of biscuits and spread with the chocolate and peanut butter ganache. Repeat these layers, then finish with a layer of biscuits. Refrigerate for at least 4 hours.

Turn the cake out onto a plate and sprinkle with broken Oreo® biscuits.

chocolate

# CHOCO PEAR
## & SHORTBREAD

20 MIN     SQUARE PLASTIC     2 H
           CONTAINER

### CAKE

250 ml (9 fl oz) whipping
cream

300 g (10 ½ oz) dark
chocolate, broken into pieces

50 g (2 oz) butter

150 g (5 oz) shortbread
biscuits, broken into large
pieces

### TOPPING

200 ml (7 fl oz) whipping
cream

5 tinned pear halves, drained
and diced

50 g (2 oz) mascarpone

1 shortbread biscuit,
crumbled

Pour the cream for the topping into a large bowl and
place in the freezer for 30 minutes.

For the cake, melt the chocolate and butter in a bain-
marie. Remove from the heat and stir in the chilled
cream until you have a creamy ganache. Stir in the
broken biscuits.

Line the mould with cling film (plastic wrap). Pour in
the ganache/biscuit mixture and refrigerate for at least
2 hours.

For the topping, using an electric whisk or a food
processor, whip the mascarpone and the chilled cream
together until thick.

Turn the cake out onto a plate. Spread the cream all over
the cake and decorate with the diced pears. Crumble
over the biscuit.

### CHEF'S TIP

For this recipe, you have to cover the cake with cream
once it has been removed from the mould because you
can't pour the hot ganache over the whipped cream in
the mould.

chocolate

# LIQUORICE
## & CHOCOLATE COOKIES

35 MIN     CHARLOTTE MOULD     4 H

### CAKE

250 ml (9 fl oz) whipping cream

100 g (3½ oz) dark chocolate, broken into pieces

150 g (5 oz) mascarpone

120 g (4 oz) cream cheese

500 g (1 lb 2 oz) chocolate cookies

### LIQUORICE CARAMEL

200 ml (7 fl oz) whipping cream

200 g (7 oz) Krema Batna® candies or liquorice fudge

### TOPPING

130 g (4½ oz) brownie, diced

a few Krema Batna® candies or liquorice fudge, cut into pieces

Pour the cream into a saucepan and bring to the boil. Remove the pan from the heat and add the chocolate. Stir until you have a smooth ganache. Refrigerate for 1 hour.

Prepare the liquorice caramel by putting the cream and candies into a saucepan. Heat gently, without stirring, until you have a creamy paste. Leave to cool and set aside.

Using an electric whisk or a food processor, whip the chocolate ganache, mascarpone and cream cheese together until thick.

Line the mould with cling film (plastic wrap). Cover the base with the chocolate mixture. Cover with a layer of the chocolate cookies, ensuring that they don't touch the sides. Spread with the liquorice caramel and add another layer of cookies. Repeat these layers. Cover with more cream and finish with a layer of cookies. Refrigerate for at least 4 hours.

Turn the cake out onto a plate and sprinkle with diced brownie and candies.

chocolate

# ROCKY ROAD

## MARSHMALLOW & CHOCOLATE

25 MIN          LOAF TIN          3 H

### CAKE

200 ml (7 fl oz) whipping cream

200 g (7 oz) dark chocolate, broken into pieces

100 g (3½ oz) butter

160 g (5½ oz) mini marshmallows

40 g (1½ oz) chocolate chip cookies, broken into large pieces

200 g (7 oz) cream cheese

200 g (7 oz) shortbread biscuits

### TOPPING

1 shortbread biscuit, crumbled

Pour the cream into a large bowl and place in the freezer for 30 minutes.

Melt the chocolate and butter in a bain-marie and stir until you have a smooth mixture. Remove from the heat and stir in the marshmallows and chocolate chip cookie pieces. Leave to cool slightly.

Using an electric whisk or a food processor, whip the cream cheese and chilled cream together until thick.

Line the tin with cling film (plastic wrap). Cover the base and sides with the cream. Add a third of the cookies, then pour over half the chocolate mixture. Cover with another third of the cookies, then pour over the remaining chocolate mixture. Finish with the remaining cookies. Refrigerate for at least 3 hours.

Turn the cake out onto a plate and sprinkle the top with the shortbread biscuit crumbs.

chocolate

# MINT THINS

## & GANACHE

30 MIN    20 CM (8 IN)    4 H
ROUND CAKE TIN

### CAKE

300 ml (10 fl oz) whipping cream

200 g (7 oz) mascarpone

60 g (2 oz) caster (superfine) sugar

3 tablespoons mint-flavoured liqueur

500 g (1 lb 2 oz) chocolate cookies

### MINT GANACHE

200 ml (7 fl oz) whipping cream

100 g (3 ½ oz) dark chocolate, broken into pieces

100 g (3 ½ oz) mint thins, cut into pieces

### TOPPING

12 mint thins

Pour the cream for the cake into a large bowl and place in the freezer for 30 minutes.

Pour the cream for the ganache into a saucepan and bring to the boil. Remove from the heat and add the dark chocolate and mint thins. Stir until you have a creamy ganache.

Using an electric whisk or a food processor, whip the mascarpone and chilled cream together until thick. Gradually whisk in the sugar, then stir in the mint-flavoured liqueur.

Line the tin with cling film (plastic wrap). Spread half the cream in the bottom, then cover with chocolate cookies, ensuring that they don't touch the sides. Spread a layer of the mint-chocolate ganache over the top and add another layer of cookies. Repeat these layers. Cover with more cream and finish with a layer of biscuits. Refrigerate for at least 4 hours.

Turn the cake out onto a plate and decorate with mint thins.

# WHITE FOREST
## CHERRY & RICOTTA

25 MIN     SOUFFLÉ DISH     4 H

### CAKE

300 ml (10 fl oz) whipping cream

450 g (1 lb) white chocolate

500 g (1 lb 2 oz) ricotta

1 tablespoon kirsch

100 g (3 ½ oz) mascarpone

40 g (1 ½ oz) caster (superfine) sugar

250 g (9 oz) shortbread biscuits

300 g (10 ½ oz) pitted cherries (fresh or jarred)

### TOPPING

100 g (3 ½ oz) white chocolate

10 pitted cherries (fresh or jarred)

Pour the cream into a large bowl and place in the freezer for 30 minutes.

Melt the white chocolate in a bain-marie. Remove the bowl, add the ricotta and the kirsch and mix well. Set aside.

Using an electric whisk or a food processor, whip the mascarpone and chilled cream together until thick. Gradually whisk in the sugar.

Put half the biscuits in the base of the soufflé dish, then add half the white chocolate cream, half the cherries and half the mascarpone cream. Repeat these layers. Refrigerate for at least 4 hours.

Shave the white chocolate for the topping and sprinkle over the top of the cake. Arrange the cherries in the centre.

### CHEF'S TIP

If you want to turn the cake out, line the soufflé dish with cling film (plastic wrap) and layer the ingredients in the reverse order, starting with a layer of mascarpone cream and finishing with the biscuits.

chocolate

# PECAN

## & MAPLE SYRUP

30 MIN

LOAF TIN

4 H

### CAKE

300 ml (10 fl oz) whipping cream

100 g (3 ½ oz) pecans

50 g (2 oz) maple syrup

500 g (1 lb 2 oz) cream cheese

80 g (2 ¾ oz) caster (superfine) sugar

200 g (7 oz) Viennese whirls

### TOPPING

100 ml (3 ½ fl oz) whipping cream

2 standard-sized Mars® bars, cut into small pieces

60 g (2 oz) pecans, roughly chopped

Pour the cream into a large bowl and place in the freezer for 30 minutes.

Put the pecans and the maple syrup in a saucepan and cook until all the liquid has evaporated. Remove from the heat when the sugar begins to crystallise around the nuts, spread out on an oiled tray and leave to cool.

Using an electric whisk or a food processor, whip the cream cheese and chilled cream together until thick. Gradually whisk in the sugar. Break the caramelised pecans into pieces and add to the cream mixture.

Line the tin with cling film (plastic wrap). Spread a third of the cream in the bottom. Add a third of the Viennese whirls, ensuring that they don't touch the side of the tin. Repeat these layers twice. Refrigerate for at least 4 hours.

Prepare the topping by heating the cream and Mars® bars in a saucepan over a low heat, stirring constantly, until you have a creamy caramel.

Turn the cake out onto a plate, pour the sauce over the top, then sprinkle with the chopped pecans.

❄

creamy

# CARAMEL
## COFFEE & MACADAMIA NUTS

25 MIN     20 CM (8 IN)<br>ROUND CAKE TIN     4 H

### CAKE

300 ml (10 fl oz) whipping cream

2 teaspoon instant coffee granules

400 g (14 oz) mascarpone

90 g (3 oz) caster (superfine) sugar

300 g (10 $\frac{1}{2}$ oz) caramel spread

500 g (1 lb 2 oz) chocolate cookies

### TOPPING

70 g (2 $\frac{1}{2}$ oz) caramel spread

50 g (2 oz) macadamia nuts, roughly chopped

Pour the cream into a saucepan and bring to the boil. Add the coffee granules and whisk vigorously to dissolve. Pour into a large bowl and leave to cool completely, then place in the freezer for 30 minutes.

Using an electric whisk or a food processor, whip the mascarpone and chilled coffee cream together until thick. Gradually whisk in the sugar.

Line the tin with cling film (plastic wrap). Spread a layer of cream in the bottom. Add a quarter of the cookies, ensuring that they don't touch the sides of the tin, then cover with a third of the caramel spread. Repeat these layers twice, then finish with a cookie layer. Refrigerate for at least 4 hours.

Prepare the topping by melting the caramel spread in a saucepan.

Turn the cake out onto a plate. Pour the sauce over the top then sprinkle with the chopped nuts.

creamy

# MONT BLANC
## SPICED CHESTNUT

25 MIN    CHARLOTTE MOULD    6 H

### CAKE

300 ml (10 fl oz) whipping cream

450 g (1 lb) cream cheese

90 g (3 oz) caster (superfine) sugar

2 tablespoons dark rum

100 g (3 ½ oz) candied chestnuts (marrons glacés), broken into pieces

100 g (3 ½ oz) speculaas (spiced biscuits)

### TOPPING

400 g (14 oz) chestnut purée

80 g (2 ¾ oz) icing (confectioners') sugar, sifted, plus extra to serve

30 g (1 oz) meringues, crushed

Pour the cream into a large bowl and place in the freezer for 30 minutes.

Using an electric whisk or a food processor, whip the cream cheese and chilled cream together until thick. Gradually whisk in the sugar, then gently stir in the rum, candied chestnut pieces and broken biscuits.

Line the mould with cling film (plastic wrap). Pour the mixture into the tin and freeze for 4 hours.

For the topping, mix the chestnut purée with the icing sugar. Taste and add more icing sugar if needed. Turn the still-frozen cake out onto a plate and, using a spatula, cover with the sweetened chestnut purée. Place in the fridge for 2 hours to partially defrost.

Before serving, scatter over the crushed meringue and sprinkle with a little more icing sugar.

creamy

# TOFFEE CRUNCH
## WAFFLE & CARAMEL

25 MIN    RECTANGULAR PLASTIC    3 H
CONTAINER

### CAKE

300 g (10 ½ oz) caster
(superfine) sugar

1 teaspoon lemon juice

300 ml (10 fl oz) whipping
cream

90 g (3 oz) butter, diced

300 g (10 ½ oz) thin waffle
biscuits

### TOPPING

250 ml (9 fl oz) whipping
cream

40 g (1 ½ oz) hard toffees,
crushed into pieces

Pour the cream for the topping into a large bowl and place in the freezer for 25 minutes.

To make the cake, first heat the sugar with 4 tablespoons of water and the lemon juice in a heavy-botttomed saucepan over a high heat, until caramelised. Deglaze with the cream and continue to cook for a further 1 minute. Remove the pan from the heat, add the butter and stir to melt. Leave to cool for a few minutes until the caramel thickens.

Line the mould with cling film (plastic wrap). Put a layer of waffle biscuits in the bottom, filling all the spaces. Pour over the semi-liquid caramel. Repeat these layers five times. Finish with a layer of waffle biscuits. Refrigerate for at least 3 hours.

For the topping, whip the chilled cream using an electric whisk or a food processor until thick. Turn the cake out onto a plate. Using a spatula, cover with the cream, then scatter over the broken toffees.

### CHEF'S TIP

For this recipe, you have to cover the cake with cream once it has been removed from the mould because you can't pour the hot ganache over the whipped cream in the mould.

*creamy*

# CHESTNUT
## & BLACKBERRY COULIS

25 MIN          LOAF TIN          4 H

### CAKE

200 ml (7 fl oz) whipping cream

350 g (12 oz) chestnut purée

380 g (13 oz) mascarpone

70 g (2½ oz) icing (confectioners') sugar, sifted

200 g (7 oz) cream cheese

30 g (1 oz) caster (superfine) sugar

350 g (12 oz) digestive biscuits or graham crackers

### TOPPING

100 g (3½ oz) blackberries

80 g (2¾ oz) blackcurrant jam

20 g (¾ oz) candied chestnuts (marrons glacés), broken into pieces

Pour the cream into a large bowl and place in the freezer for 25 minutes.

Mix the chestnut purée with the mascarpone and icing sugar and set aside. Using an electric whisk or a food processor, whip the cream cheese and chilled cream together until thick. Gradually whisk in the caster sugar.

Line the tin with cling film (plastic wrap). Cover the base and sides with the cream. Arrange a layer of biscuits in the base of the tin and cover with a layer of the mascarpone and chestnut purée. Repeat these layers twice. Finish with a layer of biscuits. Refrigerate for at least 4 hours.

Prepare the topping: purée the blackberries and the blackcurrant jam and strain through a fine sieve.

Turn the cake out onto a plate, pour over the coulis and sprinkle with candied chestnut pieces.

creamy

# SALTED CARAMEL

## & SHORTBREAD

30 MN

LOAF TIN

4 H

### CAKE

400 ml (14 fl oz) whipping cream

400 g (14 oz) cream cheese

80 g (2¾ oz) caster (superfine) sugar

15 shortbread fingers

### TOPPING

120 ml (4 fl oz) whipping cream

120 g (4 oz) dark muscovado sugar

60 g (2 oz) salted butter

50 g (2 oz) honey

Pour the cream into a large bowl and place in the freezer for 30 minutes.

Using an electric whisk or a food processor, whip the cream cheese and chilled cream together until thick. Gradually whisk in the sugar.

Line the tin with cling film (plastic wrap). Cover the base and sides with the cream. Add a quarter of biscuits. Repeat these layers three times, finishing with a layer of biscuits. Refrigerate for at least 4 hours.

Prepare the topping: heat the cream, sugar, butter and honey together in a saucepan over low heat. Stir for several minutes.

Turn the cake out onto a plate and pour over the salted caramel.

creamy

# LIMONCELLO
## NOUGAT & NUTS

25 MIN        CHARLOTTE MOULD        4 H

### CAKE

100 ml (3 ½ fl oz) whipping cream

300 g (10 ½ oz) mascarpone

120 g (4 oz) caster (superfine) sugar

700 g (1 ½ lb) ricotta

90 g (3 oz) soft nougat, cut into pieces

90 ml (3 fl oz) limoncello

zest of 1 lemon

350 g (12 oz) digestive biscuits or graham crackers

### TOPPING

40 g (1 ½ oz) liquid honey

handful of mixed unsalted pistachios and almonds, roughly chopped

Pour the cream into a large bowl and place in the freezer for 25 minutes.

Using an electric whisk or a food processor, whip the mascarpone and chilled cream together until thick. Gradually whisk in 40 g (1 ½ oz) of the sugar.

Mix the ricotta with the remaining sugar, then stir in the nougat pieces, limoncello, and lemon zest. Set aside.

Line the mould with cling film (plastic wrap). Cover the base and sides with the cream and top with a layer of biscuits. Cover with a layer of nougat ricotta. Repeat these layers, finishing with a layer of biscuits. Refrigerate for at least 4 hours.

Prepare the topping by gently heating the honey and nuts in a saucepan.

Turn the cake out onto a plate and pour over the honey and nuts.

creamy

# GINGERBREAD
## & CITRUS

20 MIN    LOAF TIN    4 H

### CAKE

50 ml (2 fl oz) whipping cream

550 g (1 lb 3 oz) mascarpone

120 g (4 oz) caster (superfine) sugar

zest of 2 oranges

zest of 1 lemon

1/2 teaspoon ground mixed spice

1/4 teaspoon ground cinnamon

750 g (1 lb 7 oz) speculaas (spiced biscuits)

### TOPPING

candied orange peel

Pour the cream into a large bowl and place in the freezer for 30 minutes.

Using an electric whisk or a food processor, whip the mascarpone and chilled cream together until thick. Gradually whisk in the sugar. Stir in the orange and lemon zest and the spices.

Line the mould with cling film (plastic wrap). Spread a quarter of the cream in the bottom. Cover with a quarter of the biscuits, ensuring that they don't touch the sides. Repeat these layers three times. Refrigerate for at least 4 hours.

Turn the cake out onto a plate and decorate with the candied orange peel.

ACKNOWLEDGEMENTS
Thanks to the whole team for their excellent work and
to Pauline, for the enjoyable and productive collaboration.

Fridge Cakes by Jean-Luc Sady

First published in 2015 by Hachette Books (Marabout)
This English hardback edition published in 2017 by Hardie Grant Books

Hardie Grant Books (UK)
52-54 Southwark Street
London SE1 1UN
hardiegrant.co.uk

Hardie Grant Books (Australia)
Ground Floor, Building 1
658 Church Street
Melbourne, VIC 3121
hardiegrant.com.au

The moral rights of Jean-Luc Sady to be identified as the author of this work have been
asserted by him in accordance with the Copyright, Designs and Patents Act 1988.

Text © Jean-Luc Sady 2015
Photography © Isabelle Kanako 2015

British Library Cataloguing-in-Publication Data. A catalogue record
for this book is available from the British Library.

ISBN: 978-1-78488-085-9

Design: Kalie+Celine  www.kalieplusceline.com
Photographer: Isabelle Kanako
Layout: Frédéric Voisin
Proofreading: Sabrina Bendersky and Véronique Dussidour

For the English hardback edition:

Publisher: Kate Pollard
Senior Editor: Kajal Mistry
Editorial Assistant: Hannah Roberts
Translator and Copy Editor: Anne McDowell
Colour Reproduction by p2d

Printed and bound in China by 1010

10 9 8 7 6 5 4 3 2 1